Your Sun, Manny

Other Books by Marie Harris

Raw Honey (Alice James Books)
Interstate (Slow Loris Press)
Weasel in the Turkey Pen (Hanging Loose Press)

(Coeditor, with Kathleen Aguero):
A Gift of Tongues: Critical Challenges in Contemporary
American Poetry (University of Georgia Press)
An Ear to the Ground: An Anthology of Contemporary
American Poetry (University of Georgia Press)

(Editor):
Dear Winter: Poems for the Solstice (Northwoods Press)

Your Sun, Manny

A Prose Poem Memoir

Marie Harris

THE
MARIE
ALEXANDER
POETRY
SERIES

New Rivers Press
1999

First edition
Library of Congress Catalog Card Number: 99:65928
ISBN: 089823-205-8
Edited by Robert Alexander
Copyedited by Louisa Castner
Series design and typesetting by Percolator
Cover portrait of Manny by Hongyu Ji (oil on canvas; 1986)
The Marie Alexander Poetry Series, number 2
Printed in Canada

New Rivers Press is a nonprofit literary press dedicated to publishing the very best
emerging writers in our region, nation, and world.

"Manny in Rincon" first appeared in *Weasel in the Turkey Pen* (Hanging Loose Press).
Versions of some of the poems in this volume originally appeared in *Longhouse* and
Compass Rose.

Excerpt from Charles Pratt, "The Road Taken," *Green Prints* (Winter 1995–96), used
with permission.

The publication of *Your Sun, Manny* has been made possible by support from Robert
Alexander; the Minnesota State Arts Board (through an appropriation by the Minnesota
Legislature and the National Endowment for the Arts); the McKnight Foundation;
the Star Tribune Foundation; and the contributing members of New Rivers Press.

NATIONAL
ENDOWMENT
FOR ❤ THE
ARTS

MINNESOTA
STATE ARTS BOARD

New Rivers Press
420 North 5th Street, Suite 938
Minneapolis, MN 55401

www.mtn.org/newrivpr

For Bill and Sebastian

For Anne and George

And for Charter, always

. . . whatever decisions you make
become fate, their alternatives
barely imaginable.

Charles Pratt, "The Road Taken"

Acknowledgments

Special thanks to all our friends and neighbors who collaborated in making a home and a haven for Manny; to all Manny's teachers and tutors, in school and out; to the poets of Skimmilk Farm; and to Sebastian Matthews, for his editorial contributions to the final drafts.

Contents

xi Preface

xiii Prologue

3 Wednesday's Child

9 Community

13 Family

17 History Lessons

25 School

35 Sports

39 Driving Lessons

43 Jobs and Money

47 Traveling Man

57 Rite of Passage

61 Rescue

67 The World Outside

75 Futures

Preface

Even now, with years of journal entries and boxes of documents to consult, I'm not sure I can really explain or reconstruct all the circumstances that conspired to deliver a teenage Puerto Rican boy to our dooryard. At the time, my husband and I were living a simple, full, and peaceful life. Then—what? The flash of a serious face on TV, the voice, the plea . . .

Many people figure in Manny's story: his adoptive father, stepbrothers, blood brother, our relatives and neighbors, his friends and girlfriends, teachers, and employers. Each would tell the tale differently. *Your Sun, Manny* is my version of the story that I have collected from various emblematic episodes into a kind of prose collage—my words, Manny's words, and other people's anecdotes, letters, reports, notes, and conversations. It is at once a personal memoir and a tribute to everyone who has taken part in this adventure, especially Manny himself.

———

Prologue

Two little boys in superhero pajamas huddle at the bottom of the stairs. They have been awakened in the night by their mother, who is shouting, shouting. Wakened in their silent night by the sound of her fists punching holes in the sheetrock. They are unable to make sense of this nightmare. All they can do is wait for her to come and coax them back into the safe dark. In time she comes.

———

She flees with them to her sister's house by train across Canada and they are happy.
Oh Annie, what is happening to me?

She brings them back home to the white house in upstate New York and they are happy.
Who's been sleeping in my bed?

She leaves for seacoast New Hampshire in a station wagon with failing brakes. And they are happy there, too.

Will anyone ever love me?

Because of a man who painted a portrait of her in a black velvet dress, she moves them to a farm in the country. He has dogs. They add ducks and goats and geese. And they are happy there.
How many mistakes do I get?

Finally she sends them away because she is overwhelmed with weariness. She hopes they will be happy there. With Daddy.

Then she finds her true love.

But now she has lost them.

Have I given you enough bread, enough pebbles to drop? Will you find your way back to me, or will crows eat the crumbs, rains wash the stones into anonymous rivers?

Women towing small children walk in the woods past my house to the houses of women with small children. I wave to them but they don't see me. I am invisible behind glass.

I walk out alone, notice a bright thing among wintergreen: blue teething ring worn smooth as river rock. Plastic clue that will never decompose.

The dreams recur. Animals tethered, then abandoned. Infants in the attic . . . somehow, oddly . . . forgotten, like dusty dolls with yellowed satin gowns and painted ceramic heads. Or torn teddy bears. *A friend says it's me, those goats and babies. She says they're the me I have neglected to nurture. But I think it's my first sons. I am drawn to the* barn's sliding doors at night; and I do mount the stairs that lead to the box-crammed top floor, shoulder up the trap door. I want to make good on the promises I made. *What were the promises? Who have I failed? What's to be done now?*

———

Charter drove me here, late at night in his old truck—the kind with a floor-mounted gearshift and a bench seat designed for a passenger to slide over close to the driver. Led me down a moonless path crusted with March snow to the one-room house he'd built by hand. *My shack in the woods.* Dinner simmered on the cookstove. There were candles and a kerosene lamp with a patterned glass shade. We fell asleep in the loft under the sounds of rain. In the morning he served breakfast in blue porcelain bowls: smoky maple syrup over white yogurt and the wild high bush blueberries he'd put up in summer.

———

Together we build new rooms with two-by-fours and sheetrock and pine clapboards.

Braced against a rib of a hip of a roof, aluminum rungs under my arches, I can see to the pond where a heron makes a pass over water like a blown cloud, and see back to the steady ladders of those afternoons when my feet found purchase on the smallest limb and I kept climbing. Now I remember something, hammer at my hip, apron full of 16-penny nails, something about being left to my own devices. (People are calling me down. The wind tangles their words. It's hard to make out who or patch together why from the shreds of their voices.)

We make summer space for little Willy to grow into teenaged Bill with his part-time jobs and paychecks and W-2 forms. For preteen Sebastian to craft an enterprise of his own . . . dried raspberry leaves and goldenrod, comfrey, mint, bee balm . . . SEBASTIAN'S SUMMERTEA.

If I have need of more, it would only be more time with them.

The temptation is to float in a green dinghy with shipped oars in ruffled water.

Snapping turtle on soaked log,
leather and crust.
Fat, guttering lotus,
flared-lipped pitcher plant
pulsing in heat.
Dinosaur toad.
Dragonfly hemming the air.

Here, without the ache and chafe of daily betrayal, of lies like black-flies at the earlobe, I could fall into a heresy of contentment.

Your Sun, Manny

Wednesday's Child

Bill is visiting on spring break. As we talk on the drive home from the airport, I find myself telling him about the one small shadow on my happiness with Charter . . . he still speaks about adopting a child, being someone's father.

Nothing more is said until the night before Bill leaves.

Go to bed, Mom. I have to talk to Charter. . . . I overhear the start of their conversation. I drift off under a silver-green moon shining through the skylight and sleep like a baby, lightly, turning and twisting until the blankets wind into swaddling cloth.

And besides, the son had said, when he'd finished talking to the man who had taught him wood and water, *you already have two sons . . . Sebastian and me. We will never leave you.*

So the husband who was not their father became a father that night. Charter said *We both cried.*

Afternoons are still warm enough for our walk through the woods to the pebbled patch by the Isinglass River where we shed our clothes and wade out to the flat rocks. Half floating in lazy late-summer currents, we sip gin and tonic from a mayonnaise jar.

Once home, Charter oils a cast-iron frying pan while I set the table. A man. A woman. Watching the last of the Boston news, waiting for the weather. As usual. Blessedly usual. Half floating in the olio of stabbings and weather, consumer updates and sports. Then this feature we have never seen. *Wednesday's Child.* And now a solemn boy who's looking right at us. I turn up the volume.

> *My name is Manny. I have*
> *never had a family and would like*
> *one . . . you know, a man and a woman.*

(Why do I turn up the volume? Why do I write down the number on the screen?)

I'm Maria, Manny's social worker.

The edges of her perfect English are softened with Spanish cadences. We are sitting at a table in a darkened restaurant off a highway in Massachusetts. Charter and Maria order coffee. My tea arrives as three separate entities: empty cup, tea bag, carafe of tepid, coffee-flavored water. She spreads sheaves of paper on the thick cloth but does not touch them.

Let me tell you what I know.

The story of any boy's fourteen years should tumble and trip over dogs and cousins and best friends, baseball gloves and birthday parties, hand-me-down bicycles, stuffed animals, crayoned drawings stuck to refrigerators with alphabet magnets, sports posters and lacy valentines from Guess Who. It ought to be filled with summer snapshots and winter report cards, ticket stubs and souvenirs, a used encyclopedia, a library card, ice skates. Instead . . .

Maria's oral history flattens the features of Manny's geography into a landscape as drear as a back alley. Born in Río Piedras, Puerto Rico, to a mother who moved to Springfield and gave him to the state as she had his older sister and would his younger brother. Then twice rescued, twice returned.

He spent a long time in a group home, and he's been in a foster home for two years. They don't speak English. We have a very hard time placing . . .

she pauses and looks at us with quiet eyes. *Certain deficits. Learning problems. No one's quite sure* . . . Her voice trails off and her hands lie still on the pile of papers. *I'll get you copies of the tests. But you should meet him. He's really special. You should meet him.*

Spanish-speaking foster parents welcome us as best they can. Manny sits on the living room couch, his drawings on his lap. A small breeze lifts the sheer curtains at the window, three flights above an abandoned parking lot, above the sounds of skateboards and someone shouting.

I love art. He speaks in English, his only language. We are at the park and Manny holds our terrier's leash and we hear birds calling.

I know my birds.

And we walk by a pond and see small fish.

Those are punkin seeds. I like to fish.

Later he sees a red car.

That's a Fiero. I like Fieros.

Charter and I drive the three hours home in silence.

Right off the bat we'd told Maria, *Look. We live in New Hampshire. There are very few dark-skinned people here. And our other children are exceptionally bright . . .*

She ignored us. Gently, politely. Because she had to do something for this boy. Time was running out. She must have sensed her opportunity when she heard us say our *other* children . . .

Maria brings Manny here in a car he likes. Charter shows him around. To the garden where late squash and pumpkins glow among withering vines. To the pond and its wooden dock and aluminum canoe, blue rowboat missing an oar, deflated inner tube and rusty bait pail. Then through the woods to the river with Adelaide bounding ahead.

It's quiet here.

Do you like that?

Oh yes. I like quiet. Noise confuses me.

The cookstove huffs. Kitchen air is apples and cinnamon. I give Maria a tour of the house. She takes notes. No mention of the outhouse. *(Why worry the bureaucrats?)* She has made her decision . . .

The phone rings and

You don't know me,

the woman begins,

> *but I had to find your number*
> *and call. I'm Manny's bus*
> *driver in Springfield. He's*
> *been on my bus for over a year*

What will she tell us?

> *and for the longest time I*
> *thought that boy was retarded.*
> *You know, he'd get on the bus,*
> *sit in the same seat, never*
> *talk, never even say good morning.*

My heart sinks

> *I felt real sorry for him. But*
> *the other day. It was Tuesday,*
> *I think. The most incredible*
> *thing happened.*

I motion for Charter to pick up the extension

> *Well, Manny got on the bus as*
> *usual, but this time he*
> *stopped right by me. He seemed*
> *taller somehow. He looked me*
> *right in the eye and he*
> *said—loud like an*
> *announcement—"I have a*
> *family, you know. I'm going to*
> *live with my new family any*
> *day now." Then he sat himself*
> *right down behind me and*
> *repeated it, like to the whole*
> *world. I mean it was weird. I*

7

mean I don't know you and your
husband, but all I can say is
from where I sit, you've
changed that boy's life.

———

When he arrives for good, he's shouldering the beige nylon suitcase Maria had given him as a present. Everything else he owns fits into one cardboard box.

———

Manny knows he's where he belongs. He walks the woods paths, as if he himself had blazed them, without map or flashlight. Any overcast afternoon. Any moonless night.

———

Boston. The TV cameras are here because this Wednesday's Child is their newest success story. The judge asks Manny some pleasant questions while we stand on either side of him. She signs him over. (Later he gets an ornate birth certificate that has him the son of Marie Harris and Charter Weeks.) Then we take him and his two Barrington best friends to the Boston Aquarium and we watch a diver feed the sharks and we see a huge blue lobster and penguins and a dolphin show and get home in time to watch ourselves on the six o'clock news.

Community

Almost no one in town calls this place a commune anymore, except from habit, though it is still an island of sorts, a colony to confound the bankers and accountants. Unconventional. That's all they might say about us now. When we leave the general store, no one whispers behind the backs of the hippies turned upstanding lawyers, nurses, contractors, teachers, businesspeople . . .

But we can still be found hammering shingles onto Wad's roof before the snow flies, pointing up the bricks on Fred's leaky chimney, stacking wood for the community house, tending Joyce's sick child until she gets back from work. We leave our doors unlocked.

Manny arrives in the dooryard like an immigrant relative. With scant knowledge of the language and customs of his extended family, slowly he learns. House by house he makes his rounds.

When he sets out, he leaves a note because we've asked him always to tell us where he goes.

(His written words—like the images he makes on the thick white paper: ceramic milk jug filled with black-eyed Susans and joe-pye weed on a dining room table in late September—are his own. The vowels . . . ah, the vowels . . . such vowels! He dips into them with his broad brush and mixes them like watercolors.)

> *Manny whent with Nicky to the*
> *Barrington basball feeld I*
> *will soon as positbale OK*
> *Chart & Mom and I did the*
> *dises and put the laundy out*
> *side on the lien OK See you*
> *soon Mom and Dad*

Jonell serves after-school tea in delicate china cups from Holland. She tells him stories about the war. *He is so sweet. Like a child. Emanuel!* Wim makes landscapes and seascapes in oil. They don't need to talk much.

> *Today is my nexst door nambers*
> *Brithday. I am making a*
> *Brithday card for him. He is*
> *geting veary old. For a old*
> *man. I am going over to his*
> *house to say Happy Brithday to*
> *Wim. He is like a grandfiother*
> *to my. I am so happy for him I*
> *like him so much.*

Arthea makes him coffee and they talk about things. Sometimes he does her dishes. Sometimes he goes down the hill to Jay's workshop and Jay lets him use his tools.

He follows a bunny path through the woods to Jennifer's house where Wes lives. Then on to Tony and Lee's where Moses lives.

He visits John now and then. And Donna. And Ann and Michael. Manny has a crush on their daughter Samantha.

Dan gets annoyed when he comes out of the bathroom to find Manny sitting on his bed, and Joyce would prefer he didn't write notes to her on the letters she's about to mail; still, they have let this be his second home.

Where are the friends?
my little boys asked long ago,
standing on an unfamiliar
porch the day of the move. I
waved in the direction of a
cluster of faculty houses and
they set out, trusting.

Wes and Mose and Josh let him come with them, fishing and camping, biking. They don't mind that he mostly listens while they talk or that when he talks he says the same things over and over.

———

I never hear him ask *What's there to do?* Perhaps he says it to himself just before he sets off into the forest or arranges to meet *Wes and Josh and them* down by the Isinglass River. He'll be wearing a purple and black bandanna and a khaki fishing vest with its pockets and pockets. He'll be carrying his fishing pole and the pail he uses for the worms he digs from the compost pile.

A late Saturday morning in the fall. Manny will be gone for hours. Long into the afternoon, I take a walk myself. Brittle brown oak leaves are noisy under my boots. I come to a spot at a widening in the river where there's an old picnic table no one uses. Today its surface is entirely taken up with broken birch branches, carefully arranged into letters. Anyone who might wonder can see that MANNY WHENT HOME.

———

There's a little boy who lives next door at Joyce and Dan's. He is seven. His name is Nicky. He loves to play catch with a football or a baseball. He loves to kick a soccer ball. His best friend is Manny. Manny plays with him whenever he wants. Then Nick grows up.

Now there's a baby in the same house. His name is Ben. Ben's mother teaches Manny how to change a diaper and how to warm a bottle. Later, Manny reads *Goodnight Moon* to Ben at bedtime. When he gets older, Manny plays catch with him almost every day. Then Ben grows up, too.

Family

Charter's father invites family to lunch when he has something serious on his mind. Today, I am his guest. Shortly after the sandwiches arrive, he says, *It is a great burden to me that my family name is about to disappear forever, as my son has no children.* (Manny of the dark skin and slow ways is not his idea of an heir.) At a complete loss, I push back my chair and leave the restaurant.

Charter's mother Louise fancies herself an artist. For a time the notion of Manny as a grandson amuses her because he paints watercolors.

Charter's sister Charity has difficulties of her own. But she is a good Auntie and picks just the right things to give him for birthdays.

———

My father likes to give children nicknames, as though he were the secret author of their lives. He named me "China" in the edgy handwriting etched on the back of my baby pictures. When his eighth child impended, he was driving, as he told it, on a highway in upstate New

York and saw a road sign that caught his fancy. *Herkimer.* Maureen was "Herkie" for as long as it took for Mom to put an end to it. So when he met Manny—our deliberate boy—Dad dubbed him "The Green Hornet." Manny wears that moniker proudly, like a patch sewn on the sleeve of a ski jacket.

My mother is the author of Manny's style. It is she who chooses the perfect fishing vest from the Orvis catalogue. She who sends him subtly patterned shirts and preppy pants. He loves her taste and tells her so. *I always look great!*

My parents have many grandchildren. Manny is but one more.

———

From me he accrues aunts and uncles and cousins by the score. But it's Annie who lends her husband and their children to Manny, understanding what we have done and who he might need . . . my next sister who well knows that family is a structure without a blueprint.

Manny's two older brothers fold him into their world as if he'd always been there. When Bill visits there are long hours of watercoloring and so many jokes that Manny learns how to make one. Sebastian takes him away to beaches and ice cream parlors where they talk about personal things. And hoop. Endless hoop in our driveway where the basket is nailed to the phone pole four inches too low.

———

Then there's José, his blood, younger brother, reluctant champion. The brother a foster family kept when they gave Manny back.

> *Come on out, José. This*
> *is where Manny lives.*

Maria's passenger opens the car door and places his city shoes on the gravel one foot at a time. His eyes dart nervously from us to our house to the forest.

He is a small, skinny figure next to this blood brother. Not similar at all. He wears his straight black hair combed back and long; Manny's is short and curly. Manny's features are bold, his skin deep brown; José's face is delicate, chiseled, pale tan.

Would you guys like a sandwich?

Please. That's Manny.

I don't care. That's José. He means yes.

He asks quick questions. He doesn't smile. As evening approaches, he keeps glancing at our big curtainless windows.

What kind of animals you got up here?

We all walk him to the car, everyone relieved but Manny.

Come up and stay here again. That's Manny.

His brother turns, hands shoved into the pockets of his black leather jacket, thin shoulders shrugged against a cold wind.

You know, you don't have to get adopted if you don't want to.
They can't make you. That's José.

José keeps visiting. His only option if he wants to see Manny. He calls on the phone. *It's me, José.* He learns how to ride the bus from Springfield and how to change in Boston.

———

We've dropped the two of them at the mall for a couple of hours. When we return, they're standing outside. José has a stricken look on his face.

There ain't no Puerto Ricans in there!

> *had a great time with my
> brouther. He came to my house
> at 11:00. I had a great
> Thanksgivening over the
> weekend. I made brifoes for my
> brouther.*

Visit by visit, José widens his world to include these woods, these people, our lives.

History Lessons

Our bedroom becomes his new room. And it becomes him, this boy who likes things shipshape.

His bed, a kind of berth cantilevered out from the slope of the roof of the house below, has bins beneath for clothes that fold and hooks beside for clothes that hang. Above, a bulb in a Japanese paper globe. Two cherry wood boards run the length of one wall for his books. Tacked to the other walls, pictures of the animals and birds he likes. They will give way to red cars and silvery jets and ebony motorcycles, be displaced by basketball posters, all studded with little school photos signed *Tammy* and *Jen* and *Crystal* and *Tiffany* and *Sara*.

Manny keeps his possessions in a metal file cabinet and in blue plastic milk crates from Scruton's Dairy. He does his homework sitting on his bed. He makes cartoons at the tilt-top drawing table with its hinged-arm lamp. He hums. Quietly, he sings all the lyrics to the music on his radio, which is always turned down low. You can hear him from downstairs, but just barely.

There are two windows. Under one, each spring, a phoebe raises up a batch of querulous nestlings. There is a skylight, Manny's private porthole to the moon and stars. From the beginning he sleeps through dawn bird racket and sleeps through the silent nights. *This is how I know what I need to know. No matter what else they tell me.*

Manuel C. Case #6073 b. 3/11/70
Bureau of Public Services, Springfield, MA, 1978
Educational Plan
Manuel needs in depth psychiatric
counseling in a stable living
environment. He needs to develop stable
personal relationships.

Children's Study Home, Springfield, MA, 1979
Referral Symptoms: firesetting,
stealing, poor peer relations, lying,
swearing, destroying property,
aggressive acting-out behavior, short
attention span.

"My name is Manny, not Manuel."

———

Manny hauls wood to feed the house fires in winter. Short wood for the cookstove. Long wood for the basement stove.

On birthdays and Christmases he gets presents from us and from Grandma in Vermont and from Annie's family in Canada. (Years later, Annie sends Manny a new wallet for his birthday to replace the one she had given him that first Christmas. It remains in its box for months and when I ask him why he isn't using it, he replies: *Oh, I can't throw the old one away. Annie and them gave it to me.*)

18

He has two kinds of skis, two kinds of skates, a skateboard, a helmet, a radio with a tape deck and speakers, the exact sneakers he likes, a box of oil paints and watercolors and several pads of paper, clothes in the colors he prefers. An allowance for posters, keychains, magazines, fishing lures . . .

. . . still he steals. Little things. Quarters from our change jar. A couple of Wesley's plastic GI Joes. (Wesley's mother calls us and we find the GI Joes and we talk to Manny and he is sorry and he writes a note about how sorry he is and how he will never.)

> *3/12/88*
> *and I need to stop tacking*
> *things from other people. and*
> *I need a lout of help Mom &*
> *Dad whut can I do to stop this*
> *prublem I need all the help I*
> *can get from you two to help*
> *me with this prublem whut I*
> *have right now OK*

Manny lies in response to direct questions, trying to divine what answer is expected.

He doesn't swear or destroy property. Nor does he act out aggressively.

> Children's Study Home
> Springfield, MA, 1980
> *Manuel is able to attend to a*
> *task for at least a 15 minute*
> *period providing the work is*
> *on his level and he is clear*
> *on the directions. He works at*
> *a slow pace and requires*
> *constant repetition. Manuel*

can perform the mechanics of
second grade math, but does
not seem to have internalized
any of the skills. He can
identify coins and their
value, but cannot accurately
count change back from a given
amount spent. He has nice
handwriting and prints neatly.
He will engage in conversation
but speaks in a low mumble.
Manny's greatest strength is
in his drawing ability.

Manny's attention span is limitless when he is fishing, roller skating, ice skating, skiing, listening to music, dancing, washing dishes, stacking wood, painting flowers . . .

Would you please go down to the garden and toss the manure on it?

The fertilizer is spread evenly on the soil as if from a tablespoon.

Could you stack this load of wood in the shed?

Maple and oak rounds are arranged in elegant patterns.

Your turn to do the dishes.

The dish drainer is a dripping still life, each saucer and cup placed just so, implements ranked by height, glasses by size.

New North School
Springfield, MA, 1982
It is possible to see Manny

*working on an assembly line
(or possibly doing something
with his artistic talent) . . .*

Manny uses a chipped white china plate to mix his tubes of watercolors. He lines up the fine sable brushes that Charter gave him. He has good paper and he takes his time. He details a pitcher of daylilies, a bucket of purple lilacs, a pot of poinsettia in green foil, bunches of basil and parsley and spearmint stuffed into an old glass milk bottle. The lines are strong. Sometimes the colors belong to the flowers, sometimes to him. Flowers are his only subject.

I like Monet best. Or van Gogh.

He paints if it is close to Christmas and I have given him a list of people who need presents from him. He paints when Bill is visiting because Bill paints all the time and Manny likes Bill. He paints evenings when homework is done.

———

*Daily performance variable.
Manuel has been introduced to
telling time.*

A milder night than the subzero weather we've been having, but cold. I've called Samantha's mother. *If you can drop them off, we can pick them up. Or we'll drop or you'll pick up or . . .* Manny listens to everything and understands something. And now it's midnight and Charter sits bolt upright in bed because he hasn't heard Manny come home, so we call Samantha's mother *(He insisted that you were coming for him)* and we call the Dover Police and we call the State Police and we get dressed and we wait and the phone rings

Is this Mr. Weeks? There's a young man here who says he's your son and he's lost.

21

and we drive to the house with the lights on and find Manny sipping cocoa in their kitchen and marvel that they'd opened their home to this dark stranger in the middle of the night.

I waited and waited but you didn't come so I started walking, and then I saw the house with lights . . .

———

Alarm permanently set for 6 A.M., he arises at wintry half-light, dresses, and creeps downstairs. Half asleep in the loft, we follow his progression by the small sounds. Clank of iron spoon on woodstove cover (rake the coals forward, lay on a stick or two to rekindle the fire). Cupboard door. Fridge door. A crunching of cold cereal. A whisper of magazine pages. Bells of silver and china and glass. Silence. I can almost hear him looking at the clock, waiting for the little hand and the big hand to come to the right place. Zipper scree. Lunch bag rustle. It takes a moment for us to realize the curtainless room is dead dark.

Manny, what are you doing?

Getting ready to go to school. (In a tone that says, Don't they know by now?)

But it's three o'clock in the morning!

Oh.

Inexplicably roused in the middle of the night, our boy glided into motion. Would he have stood four hours at the end of the road, shifting from foot to foot on hard packed snow, waiting for the roar of the bus as it rounded the corner?

———

He pulls on his work boots, grabs his heavy plaid jacket, fills the watering can at the sink, and goes out to feed and water the chickens;

returns, knocking dirt from his boots at the door, settles back to paging *Sports Illustrated for Kids,* and we all read in a companionable Saturday morning silence.

I nurse a third cup of tea, reluctant to leave the warmth of the cookstove. But it needs more wood. And the chickens could be let into the yard. I go out into the raw day.

The perpetual murmuring that usually accompanies my raking and wood carrying is conspicuous in its absence. I open the door to the hen house. The birds are strewn about the floor like so many feather dusters. I leave the door swinging on its hinges, return, knocking dirt from my boots.

Manny, did you feed the chickens? My neutral voice causes Charter to look up.

Yes. And I filled their water pan, too.

And did you notice anything? Charter puts down his newspaper. Manny brings the heel of his hand to his forehead. He is thinking.

Yes.

What did you notice? He flinches as he answers, as though to duck a blow.

They had no heads.

———

Manny comes down for breakfast. Charter is lying on the floor, knees to chest, trying to ease the muscle spasm in his back. Manny steps over him and goes to the cupboard. He pours cold cereal into a bowl and lights a fire under the kettle.

The winter holiday brings too many of us to my parents' house, so some of us are dispersed . . . to motels, B&Bs, and up the road to my aunt and uncle's house. Manny gets to stay there with cousins.

He likes his digs. The shower room with skylight. A big fireplace in the living room. A banister festooned with years of laminated ski passes hung on beaded chains.

(Later he brings this to my attention. *Mom, are they all the lost children?*)

He calls me Mom but in my heart I know we are strangers.

*Manuel is slowly coming to
terms with his feelings of
loss and abandonment.*

No. He isn't.

Everyone says: *You should have him tested. It could be fetal alcohol lead poisoning early childhood deprivation . . .*

. . . as though, having found an expert to hang a name a syndrome a cause a label around his neck like a ski pass, we could pop up to the pharmacy . . .

Excuse me, miss. Which aisle has those pills that relieve Grief and Anger? Also, we're looking for the antidote to Lack of Guilt. Oh yes, and that Cause and Effect medication. Can the pharmacist help us with the dosage? Are there any contraindications or side effects?

School

I can't handle another student!

We hear her voice through the closed door of the middle school principal's office.

*Where are we going to put him? Who's
going to supervise his program?*

When she emerges, no sign of upset.

*He'll need a series of tests
Peabody Picture Vocabulary CELF WISCR
Woodcock Johnson Vineland*

We are sitting in an empty classroom on small chairs, trying to cooperate. Later she tells us Manny was cooperative overall but

> *when he came up against too many*
> *problems he couldn't solve, he pulled*
> *his sweatshirt over his head*

and that, though his language skills are delayed by almost seven years, his understanding of single vocabulary words is his strength

> *That's a Fiero.*

although, for instance, he could not identify a bank of lit candles as a candelabra and could not come up with a sentence using the words *nothing* or *himself.*

Manny becomes a seventh grader. He picks out a plain black lunch box from K-Mart. He sets his school clothes out at night next to the little stack of penciled worksheets. Every afternoon he walks home from the bus stop. Cheery.

We light single candles at dinnertime. After homework, he amuses *himself* with music and there's *nothing* wrong.

But the school has only a windowless room and one teacher for the special kids. This will not do. So instead of staying for eighth grade, it's arranged that he "graduate" in June and enter a new school in September as a ninth grader for two years. This summer he will have a reading tutor.

> *1. Milk come from a cow.*
> *2. Ches come from cow.*
> *3. butter come from cow.*
> *6. Meet com from anoumoil.*
> *10. jeille is made of froite..*

It is as though the amplitude of Priscilla's concern requires that fulsome body, which she drapes in flowing, flowered blouses suggestive of fragrant kitchens and sunny summer mornings. From behind a long wooden desk crowded with books, file folders and stacks of lined paper, vases of wildflowers and cans of pencils, she presides over her Resource Room.

Several days into the fall semester I receive the first letter in what will become a long correspondence. It is carried in Manny's backpack—a white envelope bearing my name and, in the lower-left-hand corner: *Courtesy of Manny.* (Thirty years drop away at that moment. I can see my mother's precise handwriting on the notes that passed between her and the nuns of my childhood, dutifully delivered: *Courtesy of Marie.*):

> So, being a "new" Mom is a delightful challenge. Manny speaks so warmly about Mom and Dad. It is clear that that part of the transition has been a total success. School is going to be another challenge but one for which we all have the highest of hopes.
>
> The English class is setting up at a much lower level of literacy than I have previously experienced and this is a big plus for Manny's cause.
>
> For a while, Manny will be able to finish the daily assignments in our 8th Period study hall. I shall appreciate home-time spent on review and oral reading . . .

From that day until the June afternoon five years hence when Manny will toss his tasseled mortarboard into the stuffy air of the high school gym, school will be as much a part of my life as his.

————

We sit side by side at the dining room table adding columns of numbers, squeezing vocabulary words into whole sentences, practicing spelling. Our evening classroom includes Charter at his drafting table, absorbing grammar lessons by default. He reminds me of those bright students who, having completed their assignments ahead of the rest, get to work independently at the back of the room.

27

Night after night we struggle to make sense: Manny, of the blocky type on the pages of his reader; me, of the paths his mind chooses. I study the tight curls on his bent head. I am patient. I am the Patron Saint of Patience. I repeat. He repeats, for he, too, is patient.

One night I have to call Annie because I have hurled Manny's workbook the length of the living room. She tells me a story:

I was out on the deck with Julian the day before his science test. The more I "heard" him, the plainer it became. He hadn't studied. Spring had finally arrived. On every side, neighbors were weeding and pruning, taking in laundry. And there I was, trying to cram weeks of information into one afternoon. I snapped. They heard me. Everyone in town heard me. "Vitamin C, goddammit! Vitamin C!"

Manny pats me on the top of my bent head. *It's OK, Mom.*

And one night Manny has to write a note because he was not patient.

> *12/12/85*
> *Dear Mrs. Wilcox*
> *I am soower i yeilled at you.*
> *I will fix the moustacke.*
> *I kare about you.*
> *I well behaive in class soois I kien get good graiedss.*
> *Love, Manny Weeks*

———

Our house is filling with the objects Manny makes in Shop. A round clock with a unicorn face. A mirror with a shelf. A nightstand.

Manny is a good student. Not like those other kids.

Where did I grow up when I was little?

I grow up in Massachusetts. When i was litel boy in Mass. becus me and mi foster pariens got so mad and they hit me. becus i was get in to troubl weth my brother becus we get in to troubl a lot at home and my <u>Dad</u> and <u>Mom</u> put me in restricshun most of the day.

––––––

(Fecundo hitches a ride with a trucker out of Chicopee before day-break. He leaves his good suit in the back of the closet. At first Iris doesn't worry because he always comes back to her. But now he's been gone too long. Iris has to think. It's so difficult to think with the babies crying and everything. There's a social worker. Maybe if she gives these two babies to that social worker for a while. Yes. Then she'll be able to think better. See, when she gave away the little girl that time, Fecundo came home again. Yes.)

I live in severl diffent houses. won of the houses i live in was a partment billding. and sevrl smaler houses and a foster kare home.

Why I live in New Hampshire Now. becaus i got on T.V. with Jack wellams and we whent sailing in Boston and thas how i got put on T.V. weth Jack Wellams and i ask for a Mom and Dad becus they ran away from me. and i like the aniemals in the forest a lot. and i like to fish in the river a lot.

––––––

Priscilla holds his hand through two ninth grade years until, at seven-teen, he is beginning to inhabit some of the empty spaces, furnish them with opinions, invite people in.

––––––

In high school his teachers become my pen pals as they fill black and white composition books with assignments and notes. He takes Math Skills and English and History and Health and Biology. He takes Art but produces nothing of interest beyond a few thick clay bowls and some smudged pencil drawings. He takes Gym and Printing and Shop. His creations in wood grow larger and more accomplished. He often stays after school to help sweep up and put the tools away.

He likes all his teachers. The ones he likes best he sometimes pats on the head.

———

Sometimes friends come home with Manny on the school bus and spend the night. Sometimes he rides the bus to their houses. I speak on the phone to their mothers. They tell me Manny is a very polite boy. And helpful.

Sept 8
I like Brian he is my best freind. and we do thing togeter like __fishing__ go some were to eat twogeter sometime I spoend speand the night at his house some time. He come over to my hous to sleep over my house on Friday

Nov 11
We whent sleiding on Saturday before __dinner time__. and Rich whouned to go crous cuntree skiing over the weekend but we did not do that.

———

Manny would like to have a girlfriend. Now and then he thinks he does. I know because he draws her name inside a heart on the cover of his three-ring binder.

Sept 25
I whent out on Saturday night with __Christal__. We whent to the Fair. It was fun. We whent on the rieas. and she mad dinner for me we wouch moves on T.V. __Christal__ and I whent to the Fair.

Nov 27
and I called Jen over the weekend about going to the movies . . .

———

It is a gray, drizzly afternoon and at first I put Manny's low mood down to that. But, though he comments on the weather as sagely as any breakfast regular at Phil's Diner, Manny's take on the world has nothing to do with climate.

How was your day?

Fine.

Not his usual, *Great.* I push my notepad aside and look at him. His shoulders are rounded. He picks absently at his cuticles with one thumb. I make a pot of tea and bring him a cup.

Something bad happened. But I didn't get in trouble.

The radio is tuned to my afternoon jazz program. I rise and switch the station to his music. Music that makes me feel as though I am an unwilling passenger in the backseat of an electric-blue Camaro. Manny's fingers stop picking and begin a soft drumming.

Was it something to do with the kids in school?

Yeah.

Your friends?

No!

Other kids, huh?

Yeah. Other kids. His voice is hard. *Those other kids.*

My adult self can never quite shake youth's memories of rejection and lost loves, household upheavals, parental storms, friendships gone mysteriously awry. Empathy keeps me close.

I know how to be a mother. I've done it. Twice and more.
Because of me, Manny can say he has a mother
like the other kids. He can say

That's Marie. My mother.
I have to ask my mother.
My mother is out tonight. Can I take a message?
Your mother should call my mother.

And when they ask him what does your mother do? he can say, with some pride: *She types.*

And now, the experience I cannot share with my Puerto Rican son is the one he needs to tell. He lingers over his mug of milky tea, permitting me to quiz him. Finally . . .

They called me a nigger! He spits the sentence.

It was bound to happen, just as surely as if he had been obese or spoken with a lisp or walked with a limp. And what do I say about those other kids—the mean ones?

What do I say? I say

Manny! Look at me! Those mean stupid kids don't even know how to insult you right. You're not a Nigger. You're a Spic! His head snaps up and he looks at me, wide-eyed. Then a slow smile. The special one that spreads over his face when he gets a joke.

———

Their teachers conspired. He had no date. And she had no date. But she had a dress, a tulle dress with shoes to match. *Not light blue. More*

32

a darker blue. Darker than light. All he has to do is buy her a flower. *A corsage.* He says the word carefully, liking the sound of it. The kind that goes on your hand. He spends some time at Studley's Florist, finally settling on an arrangement of small dyed carnations in a nest of shiny leaves and baby's breath. He chooses a cummerbund that matches the flowers.

When we deliver him, Flo comes out to meet us, scattering siblings who are building a frog house near a shallow puddle. *Please come in.* Parents and relatives fill the couches and easy chairs and recliners, smoking and drinking beer. The television mumbles. We shake hands. We remark on the wall-mounted stuffed bass. Flo disappears and returns with a white box. Inside, a boutonniere of the precise shade of the flowers he now affixes to her wrist. We take pictures and repair to the lawn for more pictures. In one snapshot, an elegant young man in a tuxedo, wearing my father's pleated shirt with onyx buttons and matching cufflinks, crooks his right arm for a young woman in a gentian blue gown. Her curly red hair is pulled back in a jeweled comb. In another, the couple stands behind a row of grinning children, one of whom is squeezing a frog in her cupped hands.

Later, in the gym, under a canopy of tinsel streamers, Manny crosses the foul line, waves to the audience, slides his arm around Flo's waist, and dances away.

They will not speak to one another beyond this night.

———

Maria comes up from Springfield for his graduation. Wim and Jonell are there. The gym sparkles with flashbulbs. Red robed, Manny accepts his certificate with aplomb.

Sports

Manny loves the gear. The cleats and shin pads, the balls and bats, clubs, sticks, skis, poles, skates, goggles, hats, caps, gloves, snorkels, masks . . .

The school uniform—red shorts, red and white jersey—suits his lean body. In the photo he kneels on a green field against a backdrop of flaming maples, a black and white ball balanced on one bent leg. His curly hair is cropped close to his head and he's smiling.

Manny can run. On the basketball court he dashes back and forth at the edges, cheering whenever anyone, on either side, makes two points. On the soccer field he's a wing, loping gracefully along the sideline, shouting encouragement to both opponents and the teammates who pass the ball to anyone but him.

The parking lot is studded with station wagons and pickups. Parents sell cold drinks and steamed dogs from a handmade concession stand.

Umpires and coaches arrive from their day jobs and the kids warm up on dusty diamonds wearing shirts that say George Calef's Fine Foods and Lenzi Construction and The Christmas Dove and Landry's Auto Salvage and Knight's Garage.

Manny's team takes the field. He jogs into deep left, turns, and crouches, punches his fist into his glove. He has it down: the stance, the determined squint, flex of throwing arm, impatient pawing of one cleated foot. Innings pass. Manny lets a pop fly drop. Manny watches a base hit become a home run. Manny runs to the dugout. Manny strikes out. Manny tosses his bat with the disgust of a seasoned player in a slump. Manny returns to the outfield. When the shortstop catches the final ball, releasing his teammates to a rush for bicycles, Manny remains for a minute, posed. As if for a baseball card.

When he swims in our pond, his wake is almost as delicate as a water strider.

———

We visit my parents, his Vermont grandparents, at Christmas. All his cousins go skiing so he wants to ski, too. We take him to the hill for equipment and his first lesson.

Manny hunches over on the bench, staring at the black and green plastic boots on his feet as if waiting for information. Around him sleek women shepherd children bulging in their parkas like outlet shopping bags. Bright-eyed college students sling skis and boots onto the wooden counter. Snaps. Clomps. A young man shoves a ski pole into Manny's armpit, measures to his wrist, sends him in the direction of the red pennant—B Beginner—where a young woman in a blue jumpsuit is gathering her morning's brood. We watch them go:

the small man all in black, struggling to stay upright; three little boys crossing and uncrossing their short skis; the woman with a huge white fur hat waving her pole at someone taking her picture; and Manny tentative but looking good (*I always look good!*), moving toward the lift, standing in the way of a swinging chair that careens, catches him at the back of the knees and lofts him—skis and poles at all angles—away.

By noon the sun has softened the surface of the snow. The Vs of snow-plow turns pattern the gentle hill near the bottom.

Marie, look! Charter squints and points. Weaving among the multi-colored bodies of the fallen, skis in parallel, body bent into the fall line, a lone shape approaches. Manny ends his run in a white spray.

I don't think he needs an afternoon lesson, his instructor says. *He's a skier.* Manny starts out at the top of the mountain now.

> *Dear Garnmom and Garnpol:*
> *Thans for have me come to*
> *your hous at Xmas.*
> *Love, Your Gran Sun*

———

(Winters later he gets invited to the *Wednesday's Child* ski race as Jack Williams's guest; we three drive to the White Mountains and Manny tears down a slope and has his picture taken at the bottom. *With Jack.*)

———

He's at the far end of the frozen pond, looping and dipping, arms locked behind his back, bending and shifting on long, supple legs. To watch him skate is like following a swallow's flight.

To watch him skate! He's waltzing under pink lights and a smog of rink music, weaving through the fabric of slower couples like a tailor's needle. There's a pretty girl on his arm.

Driving Lessons

Before our Town Dump became first a landfill then a waste transfer station, I'd back up to the edge of a smoldering mountain of garbage, let down the tailgate, climb into the bed, and fling trash bags, sheetrock scraps, dead appliances, broken rakes, used tar paper, tangled chicken wire, and anything else left over from our week's labor onto the pile. Smoke of a particular, unmistakable scent drifted in the air and beer bottles exploded like muffled firecrackers.

Neighbors lingered, exchanging gossip, keeping an eye out for anything that had no business being thrown away. Not infrequently, items brought to be discarded never hit the ground. Even I was not immune. I acquired a boy's bike this way—lacking only a pedal—a pair of waders in need of duct tape and a dusty pink bathroom scale.

Ray the dump keeper knew just about everyone in town, by sight if not by name. *Good morning, Mrs. Rockefeller,* he'd shout as I eased our rusting truck to a stop.

It was our only means of transportation in those days, the 1965

International pickup Charter had driven twice across the country and twice rebuilt the engine. I liked driving it despite having to double clutch on the downshift and haul on the steering wheel for all but the gentlest turns.

Charter loved that truck. He kept its oil changed and its innards lubed. He washed it regularly and in winter took care to spray water up under the wheel wells to remove road salt. One Christmas I had the bench seat reupholstered for him.

In the summer of his sixteenth year, Bill took the wheel. Charter sat to the right of the floor-mounted gearshift and they set off down the driveway. Within minutes the truck reappeared with a fresh dent in the left front fender. Bill took a slow turn at the mailboxes and kept on turning. Into the phone pole.

Anybody hurt?

Anybody hurt? was what my Dad used to say as each of his ten children in turn sent moving vehicles off embankments, into drifts, caroming into other cars and skidding into ditches.

On a snowy Good Friday, Sebastian passed his driving test in my old blue Pinto. The following summer he was rear-ended at a red light by a licenseless, uninsured teenaged girl.

We both tried to teach Manny, but each lesson ended with him slumped over the steering wheel, defeated. Mr. Towle of Towle's Driving School had better success, though he did suggest that Manny take his course a second time. Mr. Towle wore a dark suit with a red tie. He drove a spiffy black Pontiac. Manny drove his spiffy black

Pontiac. Down dirt roads and side roads and main roads and high-ways. For six weeks. (Mr. Towle is uncomfortable with failure. In his quiet way.) And on the roads for another six weeks. Manny passed the driving test. Mr. Towle is authorized to administer the written part of the test orally should he deem that necessary. He did. Manny's license arrived in the mail.

———

The wet snow that fell last night is melting in patches. Manny drives slowly down the dirt road in the Chevy longbed we'd bought for him from a guy who owned a flooring business. He accelerates a little on the paved part. No weight in the back. Used tires. The truck begins to plane just as we reach the blind curve. When he swerves and hits the pine tree, my glasses fly off my face and Manny utters the one word he's never said in front of me.

Jobs and Money

By the time Manny graduates high school, he will have passed a dozen training courses that could have him gardener's assistant carpenter's assistant plumber's assistant veterinary assistant daycare assistant cook's assistant cleaner's assistant factory worker. He will have been taught how to read the want ads, fill out a simple application, what to say at the interview. He will know exactly what to wear and be able to explain all about good work habits.

But his crossed-out forms and mumbled interviews will never be enough. We will prevail on boss after boss to give him a try. We'll drive him to summer jobs and, after he gets his license, make sure he's on time. When he's fired for working too slowly or talking back, we'll find a different kind of a job, a new boss who might understand. When he no longer lives with us, Manny will learn about social workers and soup kitchens.

Manny likes money. He doesn't mind working for it and he's pleased when people give it to him for his birthday. If money exists in some neutral place—change jar bureau top washing machine car—it could be his. Paper money is confusing because when he pays with it he's never sure how much he gets back. Manny understands quarters.

———

Manny opens a bank account because we are teaching him to save.

———

The fair comes to Rochester's shabby north end while the days are still warm and the last of summer's breezes tease the night air.

(By day, quilts hooked rugs jams and jellies baked goods perfect ruby beets prize roosters and ducks 4-H'ers napping on hay bales beside their lambs and heavy-uddered cows. At night, harness racing rides games of chance knots of boys and skeins of girls.)

I was thinking, Manny says as he rinses his dinner plate. *Josh and them are probably going tomorrow night.* Edging toward his point. *I was thinking about going.* And Charter tells him, *Fine. Go up to the bank after school and take $10 out of your account.*

Manny puts his green savings passbook and a yellow withdrawal slip into his back pocket. *See you shortly,* he says, just the way Charter always does when he leaves the house. When Josh and them arrive, Manny comes down dressed in jeans, a short-sleeved red shirt, and a bandanna tied around his head. Charter tucks a five in his pocket. *Have a sausage-and-pepper sub for me.*

All week, each evening before supper and homework, Manny goes to the bank. Each evening, after supper and homework, Manny goes to the fair. Night after night he returns with stuffed bears and Snoopys, posters, keychains, mugs. *I won. I won again.* He gives away his loot. To us, to the neighborhood children.

And then I happen upon his bank book, the gray numbers—$10. $60. $25. $90. In total: more than $400—

Manny, how could you possibly have spent this much money?

Head bowed, shoulders collapsed, on trial . . . he can't say. So we send him to his room to think and tell the truth. And he comes back down in a while. He says: *I bought marijuana.*

This explains it.

From whom?

From Josh and them.

So we confront Josh and it isn't true and really Manny has spent his entire summer's earnings at the fair—balls and darts and hoops, rides and rides for friends, twenties handed out, change stuffed in his pocket, uncounted.

Charter looks at me and says, *He must have felt like a king.*

———

Date 10/11/89
When I get out of high school I whant to be a <u>ski instuerter</u> I like to ski a lout and I think skiing is fun to do.

10/24/89
I well be a Dad when I get out of high school. and I have to fieand a good job so I can pay <u>reant, hiet, phone</u>, for the house. I have to have a nouf money to biy gas for my truck.

Traveling Man

Where were you born?
I was born in Puerto Rico.
What is it like there?
it has poum trees alloever the
plaes. and it was sun and the
beches wher salty and the
witter was warm and it had a
lot of birdes . . .

. . . black birds and tiny, invisible frogs—*coquís*—chirping their naturally perfect sevenths. Flowering hibiscus, flamboyant trees, egrets, scuttling lizards.

We holiday there. We splash in the pale ocean, shouting like children. Bill swims underwater, one elbow a shark fin breaking the surface. Sebastian rides the waves on his belly, gulping air and salt water.

Manny changes into salsa colors an item at a time: pair of flip flops, mirror sunglasses, and a hat—a Panama-style hat with a hatband.

First thing you know our boy looks right at home, looks great in hot pink, looks around at the place we tell him he was born and he likes it, *yeah, nice place.* And when they speak to him in Spanish, he smiles and nods. Nice sounds, never mind he's nodding to the drunk in the bar who's asking him if his mother wants to dance. He drinks a *piña colada sin ron* and gets a little older, looks right. At home he looks all wrong. Wrong colors. No place for turquoise. But here it's the sky and the shutters, the sea and the store sign. Yeah. Nice.

Here we are. A makeshift family on a family trip. Having a wonderful time. Sand in the seams of our bathing suits. Burnished sun settling into pink clouds on the brink of the sea.

Bear Brook 4-H Camp

He makes neat piles of clothes and supplies, checks off each item on the list they sent. We've signed him up for one week in case he gets homesick.

Manny calls shortly into Day 4. Can he stay? (His voice says, *For the rest of my life?*)

The counselors write that Manny knows his birds and animals. He swims very well. He is polite. Also neat and helpful. He relates well to adults. He has trouble establishing peer relationships.

———

New Hampshire, Lakes Region

The summer soccer camp takes place on the campus of a private school. When he comes home, Manny says he liked it, but early on he got a large blister on the ball of his right foot so he didn't play much. But he did help the coaches a lot.

Fernie, BC

Saturday, February 25

Dearest Maz and Charter,

I got the idea yesterday that it would be neat to send a letter home for you with Manny so that you would have a fresh account of our week with him. Because Manny is not the most effusive talker, you may never hear the half of what he's done, so I want to fill you in.

But first of all I want you to know that we're all so happy to have had the chance to get to know our new cousin and we love him very much. He's been considerate, helpful, honest, funny and a big surprise in many ways. More on the surprises later.

On Sat., Manny's first day here, I hardly saw him at all because Anna had figure skating out of town. So Kirsten took him to a basketball game at the high school.

Sunday we went skiing—Anna & friend, Kirsten & friend & Manny & I. We had a blast showing Manny all the trails & runs & he amazed us with his skiing prowess.

On Mon, quite soon after the kids went to school, we dropped him off at the hill & then Kirsten & I were to meet him there in the p.m. This is quite a story . . . I told Manny to be in the lodge at 1 P.M. & we would meet him for an afternoon of skiing. Well at 1 P.M. he wasn't there. I was concerned because at this point I didn't know Manny that well & was wondering if he was lost or hurt or something. So I sent Kirsten off skiing with a friend while I stayed near the bottom of the hill looking for Manny. Anyway, around 2 P.M. I spotted him & he was nonchalant & fine. When I asked him where he was at 1 P.M. he said "skiing." Well, I was kind of mad because I had been worried & I remembered your words that if he screwed up give him heck. So on the way up the chairlift I start this lecture about . . . "how do you expect me to let Xavier miss a half day of school to ski with you if you can't be in a certain place at a certain time etc. etc." As Manny's head is drooping lower & lower & I'm feeling like a real shit, I start to wonder whether he might have trouble telling time—so I ask him what time he has & he says 3:15. Guess what? It was actually 2:15! Because of the

49

time change from East to West, Manny had reset his watch, but not by enough. Boy did I feel bad. Then when I questioned Manny some more he had actually been at the lodge at 1 P.M. his time & we weren't there. Can you believe it?

On Wed Xavier took the day off school & skied with Manny. There were also 22 kids from our school & 22 kids from Quebec at the hill because this was the week of our "French Exchange." That night Xave & Manny went out with some of the kids to the arcade & then to someone's house to watch a movie.

Thurs. night was the school dance & that's another one of Manny's surprises. Here I am worried that he might not have fun & I have Xavier assuring me that if Manny looks unhappy he will walk home with him, & what happens? Xave & Manny get invited to a party after the dance & don't get home til midnight at which time Xave bursts into our room to tell us that Manny was the best dancer in the place, never sat down for a minute, & was the total hit of the night! Manny's face was beaming as he says, "Yeah, I'm a good dancer." The only kids who came close to his dancing ability were the Quebec students which says something about Easterners. Oh, the other thing Xave said with a twinkle in his eye was that Manny dances so well because he's a "brother"—and Manny echoes—"Yeah, I'm a brother." I tell you.

Some of the Manny surprises . . . his great voice and his knowledge of all the words to all the songs, his skill on skis, his incredible dancing, his independence, his ease with people, his appreciation of hockey and figure skating, his beautiful smile, & his quiet self-assurance.

As for homework. Well, whenever our kids did homework, Manny read, which I figured was good. He got into *Charlotte's Web* & he really enjoyed reading it. He did a math worksheet one night but I didn't push that. After all, it is his holiday . . . .

Well now it's Sunday, our last day with Manny & Kirsten, & we'll certainly miss them both. One last day of skiing, one last dinner, and a nice drive to the airport. We hate to see the week come to an end.

Please think about the summer & convince Bill & family & Bash that their coming too would make everything perfect.

Love & xxxx
Annie, George & the gang

We find Manny at the baggage carousel waiting for his skis, hockey skates slung over one shoulder, duffel bag at his feet. Instead of smiling when he sees us, his eyes fill with tears. He begins to speak incoherently.

It's OK, Manny. We're here. We'll get a coffee for the ride and you can tell us what happened. It's OK. You're home now.

Apr 07 1989

Senator Warren B. Rudman
United States Senate
Thomas J. McIntyre Federal Building
Portsmouth, New Hampshire 03801

Dear Senator Rudman:

Reference is made to your letter of March 15, 1989 in behalf of Charter Weeks concerning the immigration inspection experienced by his adoptive son, Manny Weeks at Toronto, Canada pre-flight inspection on February 27, 1989.

Our records indicate that at the time of his application for admission to the United States that Manny Weeks was unaccompanied. He stated that he was a United States citizen and for identification presented a New Hampshire driver's license and a copy of a Puerto Rican birth certificate, which is a document notorious for being used to fraudulently claim United States citizenship. Since he was unable to answer some routine basic questions about his country of birth, although he claimed to have lived there for nine (9) years, he was referred to another inspector for additional questioning.

This is our normal operating procedure. Manny's race was not germane to the issue, only his lack of information about certain routine questions posed to him. Also, no thought was given to Manny being retarded since he had traveled back and forth across the continent alone and had a valid driver's license. Our review of this matter fails to reveal that our officers or supervisors acted in a racist manner, or that their actions were other than routine given the circumstances. Manny was not treated in a rude, discourteous or humiliating fashion. He was only questioned regarding inconsistencies of his responses to questions concerning his place of birth and citizenship. This line of questioning is required by our officers not only to prevent the entry of malafide applicants, but also to identify runaways or other minors ticketed for travel who should instead be intercepted and returned to their parents or appropriate social service agencies.

We sincerely regret the anxiety and discomfort experienced by Manny and his parents as a result of his inspection. We hope our response better clarifies for Mr. Weeks the events that occurred. In the future, should Manny have occasion to depart and return to the United States unaccompanied, it is suggested that he be provided with a letter from his parents briefly outlining his travel itinerary and other particulars, including a telephone number to call in the event a problem arises.

We hope the above information will be of assistance to you in responding to your constituent.

Very truly yours,

Benedict J. Ferro
District Director

March date 3/6/89
Dear Annie, George, Xavier, Anna Kirsten. I thank you for have me viseat you people. I well come and viseast in the sumertiem. and I like the skiing mountones it was fun to ski in CANADA. The school was nice I like a lout. Thankes for the prisezes Anne and George. I well oppen theam when my brithday comes. I meies you people a lout. I well see you people in the summertime OK
See you Annie, George,
from Manny Weeks.

March date 3/6/89

1 Dear Xavier: I had fun with you wheh I came to see you people. I had fun a the school daince on Thursday night.

2 Tell Tammy that I had fun daiening with her on Thursday night. I had fun thank you Xavier.

3 Tell Tammy I whount to go out with her OK. She is a nice gril Tell Tammy I well see her in the <u>sumertime</u> she is the best and the <u>nice gril</u> I have daiecn with in the school. Tell her I mies her so much.

4. and Xavier send me a litter soon Xavie. and Xavie give me Tammy'es addres so I can right back to her.

5 Thank you for the picher you gave me. I need a picher of Tammy.
and Xavie did you take to her about me did you tell her whunt I told you have fun playing hocky OK Xavier
See you Xavier. right back soon OK I whunt to hear eveathing about it.

———

Outward Bound

In my mind I see you, standing quietly beside your pile of gear while everyone around you is talking talking. And then the vans and the drivers and the checklists and you follow. But now you've found the young man who's leading the expedition and you help him load packs onto the roof rack while the other kids are jockeying for the best seats and arguing over something you don't understand or care about because you want to make sure everything's OK like the straps and the door latches and you sit beside your friend and you don't talk because the young man has fallen asleep on your shoulder.

The Boundary Waters. Before you left, we located that cluster of pale blue shapes on the map, a knotted scarf of lakes between Minnesota and Canada. That's where you are now. In a canoe. Or portaging around rapids. Or in a tent. And it's beginning to rain. Or the morning sun is knifing the ground fog. Or the moon is rising between stark black pines.

The Test. They drop you off on a spit of land with a tarp and some matches and whatever you have stowed in your fishing vest.

I'm not worried, Manny. You know your birds and berries. You know your fish. You know that the owl is not hunting you at night. You know the deer can drink, undisturbed by your presence, and the otters will play as if you were not there. This is your territory. You have never been afraid of the natural dark.

The Flight Home. Has been delayed by a storm. I'm worried now, Manny.

The Minneapolis airport is noisy and you've never liked noise and the young man has said good-bye and you haven't quite caught his last instructions so you shoulder your damp gear in the general direction but you don't exactly know and you won't ask and you miss and you wait and while you're waiting you think about otters diving and how, when your test was over, someone came and took you back to camp and offered you a bowl of stew.

———

Seattle

Friday 1/19/90
I am going to see my briether
name Bill for a week. I mess
him so much. he is my
briother. So is Basten. We
play baskitball.

I put him on the last plane out of Logan before ice and fog closed down the show. If he doesn't leave, we don't go on holiday.

(Bill told us he arrived to more snow than that city had seen in years.)

Manny has a good time with his brother Bill. He keeps telling the girls they ought to help their mother more. And not fight so much. He does dishes all the time. And homework. He paints a lot with his brother Bill.

Charter and I have many wonderful holidays. Just the two of us.

Rite of Passage

I can't go home anymore.

He has never defied us. Now this. I was away. I hear it when I return

His father's decision not to allow him to drive to Robert's over icy March roads. His disappearance with the truck into the night. And gone the next night and the next. Not far, but, it turns out, far.

It's Sunday. About time to fetch Manny home. Charter goes. *(Should I have?)* But he doesn't want to come. And Rob calls the cops because Rob is accustomed to calling cops and the cop arrives as Charter and Manny are getting into the car and he says *What's going on here* and he says *Is this boy over twenty-one and if so he can do whatever he wants* and Charter says *You don't understand* but the cop doesn't care to understand and Manny says he wants to stay so Charter leaves without him.

Now I'm in the Barrington Police Station, which shares its space with the Public Library. It's noon. Rob and Manny are slumped in orange plastic chairs in the waiting area. The Chief says *Why don't you and*

Manny go into the other room where you can have a private conversa-tion. I ignore Rob. Manny and I go in, past a plastic NO SMOKING sign and I glance at the Chief, who shrugs. But in a few minutes there's a knock on the door and a young officer delivers an ashtray.

Manny is clenching and unclenching his fists, grinding his knuckles into his forehead. His words come out on shallow breaths. He is suffering. I cajole. I empathize. I question. I am gentle. I am stern. It's no use. I am trapped in a small room with an implacable stranger who says over and over, *I can't go home anymore.*

OK, Manny. Do what you need to do, but I'm going to have to take the truck is there anything you need out of it? And Manny thinks and then he says the radio and I say *I'm afraid the radio goes with the truck* and I leave the both of them, Manny and Rob, to figure out how to get wherever it is they're going next.

Manny shows up around five o'clock. *I've come to get my stuff,* he says. And I say *How did you get here* and he says *Rob and them. They're waiting for me at the mailboxes.* And I think good thing they don't dare show their faces here. And Manny goes up to his room and turns on the radio. Half an hour. An hour and still the music and the sound of drawers opening and closing. (I don't say, *Hurry up, your friends are waiting.*) Manny's humming. Another hour. Finally he comes down lugging two suitcases, his red string laundry bag, and the stuffed Tasmanian devil Charity gave him. *Bye, Marie. Bye, Chart.* As though he were off to 4-H camp. He hugs us.

After he leaves, I retrieve the green passbook—almost seven hundred dollars Manny had saved up—and toss it into the woodstove. I won't make it easy for him to bankroll his friends.

———

9:45. The law arrives in our driveway, blue lights flashing, followed by a beat-up vehicle. *Your boy here wants to get his bank book.* It's gone, I say. *Oh,* says Manny. *Go on,* I say. *Good-bye, Manny.* The officer leaves us his card and Manny returns to the beat-up vehicle. They pull out.

Whatever we have managed to teach him is all he has now: a kind of cardboard box filled with souvenirs of a family life.

————

(Adelaide—game terrier of happy memory—chose an invisible line beyond the hand pump, halfway between house and woods. Up to that point she would hear us calling and so have to return; past that, she went deaf and proceeded on journeys of her own devising.)

He will come home. And leave again, though no further than the next town over. He will inhabit shabby rooms on second floors over unkempt yards littered with automobile parts and broken bicycles. We will help him furnish bedrooms and living rooms, stock kitchens with pots and plates. He will sell his furniture, abandon used televisions and crusted frying pans. He will have jobs and he will be homeless.

————

José moves up from Springfield, leaving behind a girl and their child whose photo he wears as a button on his jacket. For a time they live together at 47B Ham St., Dover, but José tells him what to do and Manny is the older brother so that doesn't work and José moves in with his new girlfriend. The place fills up with underage kids who get Manny to buy their beer and cigarettes at the corner store.

He gets fired from his job at the nursery, evicted from the apartment. He goes from friend to friend. It's summer and we stop intervening.

There's this place, Marie. A church. You just go there and they give you dinner. (And your parents pay them back.)

Rescue

It's almost September. Manny's still eating at soup kitchens.

The application has been in at the Job Corps for almost a year. The weeks drag on and still no word. Now a new Job Corps person calls with her revised agenda. She says she's reviewing the applications. She wants it all again . . . the IEPs, the psychological evaluations. *It's possible that his disability will disqualify him.*

Who do we know? What can we do?
No one. Nothing.

I surrender to sleep reluctantly, scrolling down my random access memory

which delivers the answer at dawn. *Sargent Shriver.* He'd written my mother a note when Dad died. She told me they'd been friends long ago.

Perhaps they'd danced to the music of Lester Lanin at some cousin's debut party and he'd wished, for a moment, that he might stay in her arms forever. Or maybe they'd ridden horseback together across a mown field, knee to knee. I don't know. That was so long ago. Such a different time. So much simpler.

I send a letter and three watercolors. He writes back.

It's always a pleasure to hear from you and your family, although, sad to say, I have had many, many too few communications. Most of all, I am impressed by what you are doing, by what you would like the Job Corps to do, and by the lucid descriptions you give to Manny's accomplishments and needs. . . .

Now for the specifics of your request, here's what is already underway . . .

. . . But if you don't hear from them quite soon, please don't hesitate to call me. I have very good relations with the leadership of the Job Corps and am not at all unwilling to badger them a bit in order to find the best way in which to provide the most appropriate training for Manny.

This letter brings you and your husband my best wishes. I am glad you wrote to me.

Sincerely yours,

The day after Manny is accepted into the program, a secretary from Mr. Shriver's office calls. *Is everything OK? Can Mr. Shriver be of further help?*

No, thank you. Everything's fine.

I refer back to his letter.

P.S. Incidentally, Manny's artwork is superb. When I first looked at it, I thought it was by van Gogh.

Van Gogh, I add, is Manny's favorite painter. After Monet.

Manny takes their list upstairs and circles and stars and checks and underlines. He folds two of this and four of that; chooses which T-shirts and sweaters and pants, what tapes and magazines. He's leaving home again and he knows how to pack. Humming along to his music.

We three ride up the Maine Turnpike to Bangor. When we finally find the place, a cheery dorm counselor tells us that this Army barracks is temporary so we shouldn't worry about the peeling paint and the toilets with no seats and the graffiti in the stairwells because the new campus is almost ready, so we settle Manny in and take him out to dinner and say good-bye and good luck.

> Date
> *10/10/93*

> *Sunday's note*

Dear <u>Mom</u> and <u>Dad</u>: I am haveing a somewhut time here at the <u>old</u> <u>Dorm</u> It is getting vear bad at this places And I miss <u>Dover N,H</u> so much. (.And <u>Mom</u> and <u>Dad</u> I got my Class "A" Pass at the old dorm.) And also I got two pices of paper from the job corps Center (.And I am vear happy albout it albout the job I have ben doing in the job Corps Center.) And I got three thinges I did gerat on in the job corps Center.) (.And I am doing all the things in the old Dorm Mom and Dad
(.And I heard a lout of bad thinges in this place Mom and Dad.)
(.And thay are <u>druges,</u> and <u>people geting into fiteing with people</u>.) And thas how I do not like this places <u>Mom</u> and <u>Dad</u>.)
I rather get a job in now N,H, like <u>Dover N, H,</u> whear my Bruother José is right now <u>Mom</u>.) (.And Mom I am going to send you this thing of paperes in the mayol OK Mom and Dad
Hi! I miss you two so much
And I miss my bruother José alout

Thresday night note
Date 10/14/93

Dear Marie Harris: I am haveing a bad time whear I am. (And I whunt to go home and stay thear in Barrington, NH on Thankesgiveing for good.

And Mom I need more monye $

But before Thanksgiving, before we must rescue him, he moves into the new campus with its lighted paths, its gym and cafeteria, the girls' dorm and the boys' dorm . . .

Just like college. Just like Bill and Sebastian.

Satrerday 11/20/93

. . . and tell Nick that I am doing veary great in the job Corps Center in Bangor M.E.

On our next visit, he shows us his spiffy dorm room, introduces us to a roommate and a dorm counselor, takes us on a tour. Wherever we go kids say *Hi, Manny* and *How's it going, dude.*

He gets a paycheck and bonuses and special privileges, passes courses in Building & Maintenance, earns Certificates of Excellence. And a girlfriend.

At first he comes home on the Trailways bus for holidays. But soon he's calling to ask if he can stay. For Easter. Then Fourth of July. For Labor Day and Thanksgiving. *They need me here.* Until his whole life is in Bangor *with my teacher Mark and them becaus we're making a gazebo and we're helping to put staers on an old ladys house and we're going up north to work on something and I and I'm doing veary good in my woodshop class, Mom and Dad, and I will give you two pichers of*

what I am doing in my class. Love, Your Sun
for two years. And then it's over.

I'm a few minutes late to meet him at the bus station in Portsmouth. He's standing on the sidewalk among a pile of duct-taped boxes, smoking a cigarette. His sadness is such that he can hardly speak on the drive home.

The World Outside

The blue '86 Chevy step-side truck is his Job Corps graduation present. With it he can drive to a job that he'll surely get, what with his enthusiastic letters of recommendation, his new skills. And make extra money on weekends doing odd jobs if he wants.

The studio apartment should be just right. We shop for a used TV. New cutlery. A bed and a red beanbag chair. Manny buys the paper every day and puts circles and underlines on the Help Wanted page. Randomly.

We know someone who needs a carpenter's helper.

A few months later we know someone who knows someone who has a business cleaning offices and banks at night.

————

I convince myself that we've launched him.

Fresh paint on the upstairs bedroom walls—white with a trace of green, a subtle color that simmers like a fish tank when afternoon sun fills the skylight. The Chinese screen—torn in places and faded—that my grandmother Mimi brought back from one of her steamer-trunk journeys abroad, unfolded to cover the closet pole. My clothes on the pole. New paintings to replace the basketbull posters. My books on the shelf and the brass lamp on the bedside table that lit my bedside when I was young.

Our son Manny is always welcome to sleep in this room. As a visitor.

It's going wrong. Manny waits for Mark to phone from Bangor, telling him he can come back to work at the Job Corps. He begins drinking.

Penny calls. She's seen some kids driving Manny's blue truck around Dover. She's heard that Manny's sold it to them. Charter and I drive out into the hot, damp night to search the streets for the house that Penny described.

A skinny man in an undershirt opens the door partway. *That's right. I gave your boy $150. I have a bill of sale. All legal.* Can we come in?

Because I'm fuming and no use as a negotiator, I stay in the front room where the TV blares and a clutch of half-dressed children are climbing around on a torn sofa. A toddler sniffles and whines with fatigue.

Charter continues through to the kitchen, sits down with the man at a Formica-topped table. Five glassy-eyed teenaged boys balance on the backs of chairs, grinning and nudging like spectators in the bleachers at a cockfight. The document is produced: a page torn from a 1987 Dover High School yearbook with terms and two signatures scrawled on the back. Charter talks quietly. Talks reasonably. Talks for a long time. A solution is arrived at that involves our money. He puts in a call to the cops and presently a police officer, wearing shorts and a holster, shows up on his mountain bike to witness the handing over of the keys. *All legal.*

I shift the sleeping child from my lap to a pillow on the rug and we leave. The boys follow us to the street, mocking.

———

Manny moves in with Penny and her boyfriend but he won't pay her for rent or food and she calls us daily to complain about the money and the booze and she can't understand because she's been good to him . . .

He gets a job in a shoe factory. Quality Control. Jonell gives him her old car. He moves in with an old lady who keeps parrots and dogs and cats in every room of her house. In winter they cause him to wheeze. We hear about him from José or Penny.

Manny takes up bowling. He pays for pool games at a social club for recovering alcoholics by sweeping the place on Saturday afternoons. He goes dancing at Pure Platinum and buys drinks until his money runs out.

I'm on my own now. Manny doesn't need us anymore. Except for wisdom teeth, tax forms, car repairs. Etc.

———

In the courtroom, on wooden benches, three women fidget as if they were early arrivals at a baptism. One of them has snapshots of a baby tucked in her purse. (She tells me this in a whisper.)

Manny and I are in the judge's chambers. The judge is speaking slowly, deliberately. *Manny, do you understand the meaning of the word* oath?

Manny thinks.

How old are you? Where did you go to school? Are you a good driver?

What's your job? Do you know a young lady called Kimberly? Did you have sexual relations with her?

I had picked Manny up at the shoe factory. He hadn't shaved and his work clothes smelled faintly of glue. Now I want to tell the judge that Manny is a good dresser, a boy who looks after himself. I also want to say he's a painter of flowers in the manner of van Gogh. I want to speak his answers for him because words come slowly to Manny and he tells people what he imagines they might want to hear. But I remain silent.

Manny rarely lifts his head when he's being questioned. About anything. He never knows. Better to wait until they tell him what to say. But there are some things about which Manny has no doubts. No doubts at all.

I am a very cautious driver! he announces, looking up.

When it is all over, Manny signs his complete formal name in cursive on the line and, with the judge's permission, adds the date. The judge asks if he has any questions and Manny says yes.

I've been thinking. Will the child's new parents take care of him and make sure that he will be able to be on his own someday?

Out in the parking lot, Manny says *that was nervous wracking* and he says, again and again as is his habit, that he had been thinking a lot. And I tell him that one of the ladies in the courtroom told me that the little boy has new parents who love him and they go to church and Manny thinks that's good. And then I say *would you like to have a coffee* and he says *sure* and we stop at a pizza place in Gonic and Manny says *I've passed this place lots of times on my way home from work and I never knew it was here* and we look at their fish tank and I say *we've seen some of these fish in the Caribbean* and he says *Puerto Rico is the Shining Star of the Caribbean* and then he orders a small chicken sub and we talk about AIDS and condoms and not having children by mistake and I drop him off at his car in the shoe factory parking lot and we hug and he says *thanks Mom*.

This is Cyndi? Manny's new girlfriend?
Are you his mother?
Do you take children?
I heard you take in children?

No, Cyndi. I know what you're thinking, though. This lady and her husband took in Manny. I know. Manny told Penny and Penny told me all about it. This lady and her husband do adoptions and I have three kids and I think I'm pregnant again and I can't I can't I can't. This lady could take all my kids and I could start again and Manny could be my boyfriend and we could go to the club and we could dance all night.

Summers ago we all converged on a level spot in our woods behind Tony's house and in a weekend built a cabin for his mother without benefit of building inspector or permit. Pine-simple as our own first dwelling. A place where she could read and sleep, eat and drink red wine. Away but close enough.

Charter tells me I would regret it if we were to make such a cabin for Manny.

———

Esquire *magazine rounded up a few bums in that time when they were still bums, not The Homeless. A bevy of bright young women trimmed the beards and styled hair, decked them out in tweeds or evening wear, accessorized (silver-tipped cane, ascot, beret, the single red carnation), and posed them (one, whose teeth were beyond repair, directed not to smile) against the backdrop of privilege. Perhaps they enjoyed fine coffee and good port, smoked Cuban cigars and made long-distance calls before they were returned to the streets. I wonder if they were permitted to keep the new clothes.*

Manny used to wear gray slacks and blue blazer, white shirt and muted striped tie for funerals and weddings. In summer, the same outfit without the tie, shirt open and a vest, a pair of soft leather shoes and sheer black socks. He could converse with strangers, gracious, relaxed against any backdrop.

We keep these clothes in a zippered plastic bag—tie looped on a hanger with the vest—for when the next family member marries. Or dies.

In the attic, his skis and ice skates, roller skates, skateboard. Some of his paintings, shrink-wrapped. A baseball bat and mitt. Soccer cleats.

Our other sons have stowed boxes here as well. To reclaim. So why do I look at Manny's stuff and think: Goodwill.

He hasn't been the same worker since Tony left. The new boss has given him three warnings so far. We have no choice but to let him go.

———

Jennifer calls. *Can I come over?*

A month ago when I was away Manny came by and he left a note as he always does about how he hoped I was having a good time. Signed Your Friend, Manny C. Weeks. And now I get this canceled check made out to him for two hundred dollars and signed by me. It looks just like my signature! Did I write him a check?

Some time after Manny has finished scraping the paint around her storm windows, Nancy is missing her silver spoon. *By any chance?*

Joyce calls, apologetic. Manny has been helping her with some chores. There's a gold chain gone from Lena's room and the money she was saving for her trip. *Could it be?*

On a hunch, we unearth Charter's coffee can, the one he stashes, chipmunk fashion, in a hole in a boulder to hold the hard cash he's certain we'll need when everything falls apart. It's empty. *Is it possible?*

that our Manny has been a one-man robbery ring?

Caught. Confronted. He is sorry. He writes notes to everyone saying he is sorry. He decorates them with pictures and signs them *Your Friend, Manny.* For he is our friend Manny. He is safe with us.

(a) Stealing is when people take money from them and you get in deep trubol that you end up in jail.
(b) NO it is not good to take a little becuas you will get a puneshment when you steal ageen from your family.
(c) if you tak anneything from your friends they will not like you as a frend for a lung time.
(d) Becuse it is a bad habit to steal becus you will get into so much trubol from your family.
(e) If i need money I shud aske my Dad or Mom for sume money. or i can get money out of the bank.

Joyce installs locks on her doors for the first time in twenty-five years; her family has problems remembering where the keys are. Jonell watches out for Manny's truck and stops asking him to tea. Jennifer makes it clear he is no longer welcome in her home.

Tonight Manny arrives with his payback installment. I fix him an iced tea. We have a chat about the weather.

Then he pulls out a set of shiny keys on a round plastic Blue Seal key ring and sets them on the table. He tells us that he's gotten his car keys copied, just in case. Something to praise him for. And we praise him.

In order to keep our brief conversation alive, Charter tells him about the moose he and Wim saw swimming across our pond the other morning and he says *now that's unusual* and he says *I saw Jonell on my way in and I waved.* He finishes his drink and the menthol cigarette he had tucked behind his ear and is on his way.

(This is how it would go if I ran the circus. There'd be a woman.

Let's say her name is Cheryl. She's thirty-three and has two preschool children by a man who abused her. She's finally got free of him. I have him out of jail and moved to another state somewhere in the Midwest. She holds down a good first-shift job at a plastics factory and the kids are in a day-care situation she trusts.

Cheryl grew up in a small town just across the border in Maine. Her parents love her and feel helpless, sometimes. Every other weekend they take the kids so she can have a night out.

One Saturday Cheryl sees Manny at the bowling alley. She likes looking at him when he bowls. His long legs and easy arm. He notices her watching and invites her to bowl a string or two. She helps him with the scorecard and then they have a beer. Understand that Cheryl is in no hurry to add another man to her life, but then Manny . . .

well, he takes to dropping over and he's content to play with her kids for whole afternoons while Cheryl cleans house and then she asks him to stay for supper and he does up the dishes afterward and she begins to like him all the while realizing that there are certain things Manny doesn't do too well but, after all, she knows how to balance a checkbook and Manny does get those kids to sleep faster and easier than she ever could and he's patient and quiet and loving and . . .
well, you get the picture.)

Futures

He wouldn't take off his coat or hat, his Aunt Charity says, *but he accepted a cup of coffee and then he told me very politely that it was the worst coffee he'd ever tasted. I think he had come for a birthday gift so I chatted with him and presently wrote out a check for ten dollars, expecting him to take it and leave.*

But instead he took off his baseball cap and unzipped his jacket and asked for another coffee with extra milk and sugar. We talked for quite awhile then. You know how deaf I am in my left ear and Manny speaks awfully quietly but what I heard had to do with friendship and loneliness.

These days, Manny's drinking less. Still living up the road in the old lady's farmhouse with her caged birds and feral cats, the barking dog chained to its plywood house, chickens, geese . . .

. . . she washes his clothes and asks nothing of him. *I just love him to death. I wake up when he comes home late and I make him eggs and bacon. They tell me I'm crazy to do it, but I like to . . .*

and he doesn't pay for food or rent. Now and then he mows her lawn or shovels the driveway.

———

Manny's showing up here more and more. He rakes the yard clean of oak leaves, hauls them into the woods, pile after pile in a blue plastic tarp, using an ingenious knot system that permits him to shoulder an Atlas load as if it were a knapsack, as if he were not Sisyphus. And he says *Chart, I think you need help stacking that wood.* And he says *The mulch I got for your garden looks good, Mom.* And he says *Dads and Moms are lucky to have sons to help them.*

———

My mother had a baby every two years. She cried when she told me she was pregnant with her tenth, but only for the moment it took her to compose her beautiful face. When any of us—especially me, who pounded my fists against her implacable acceptance of all things traditional, ecclesiastical, and male—asked about regret, she would respond: *imagine if there were no Basil, no Peg or Maureen or David, no Charlotte!* and we would try, unsuccessfully, to erase a sister, a brother from our lives. It wasn't fair, that argument, but it worked for her then as it works for me now. Suppose there were never such a thing as television and, therefore, never a couple watching a TV segment called *Wednesday's Child* while one was washing up the dishes as the other prepared the evening meal. Suppose there were no such thing as a telephone or a toll-free number or free will. It would be like imagining that Manny was never born.

He's sipping a cup of tea with honey and lemon the way he knows I fix it for myself. He's come to borrow money against the paycheck he'll be getting for the new job he's landed all on his own washing dishes in a restaurant in the mall *for a lady boss starting Monday 5 to 9:30.* Charter says *Great. You're really getting good at making it on your*

own. We're proud of you. Then we start talking about the spotted sala-
mander he and I saw yesterday, which starts Manny on a little reminis-
cence about one he saw in the woods a long time ago. We get out the
book and he says *yes, that one,* pointing to the Marbled Salamander
and he goes on, as he will, about how he said to himself *hmmm, what's
this?* etc. I ask him if the dentist took out the wisdom tooth stitches
and that leads him into a memory riff about the other infected wisdom
tooth that had his right cheek swollen and his eye almost shut and how
*the dentist said it's a good thing I caught it in time otherwise you could
have had serious brain damage.* We give him a tall bottle of the maple
syrup he watched us make last week and he takes one of our Post-it
notes and writes <u>Dad wood stacking 10:30</u> and affixes it to the bottle

and suddenly I realize just how much I have come to love this boy who
signs his notes to us

Your one 3thred sun Manny.

Manny hesitates at the screen door
comes back to hug us
and goes out into that long day
he awakes to every morning
as surprised as if it were
the very instant of creation
sudden and inexplicable
a world with nothing in it to regret
nothing
to change or predict

Marie Harris is the author of three volumes of poetry and editor of several anthologies of poetry and literary essays. Her travel articles have appeared in newspapers and magazines ranging from the *New York Times* and *Boston Globe* to *American Cemetery* and *Corvette Fever*. She has worked as poet-in-residence in elementary and secondary schools throughout New England. She has served on the New Hampshire State Council on the Arts and is a Trustee of the Barrington Public Library. Marie Haris and her husband, Charter Weeks, are partners in Isinglass Studio, a business-to-business advertising agency.